to the memory of my grandmothers,
who led by example, and showed us the joy of the kitchen

50 VEGAN SALADS

REUT BARAK

CONTENTS

INTRODUCTION

I've always had a love for new recipes. I started cooking when I was seven. The first thing I made, all on my own at the age of seven, was Challah bread. I was brave. The result was what could only be described as beginner's luck.

I have since had every possible failure in the book...and some of my own. But I always succeeded in the end, and over the twenty-five years I spent in the kitchen, I learned how to cook. I learned that when you burn a pancake, you are not making a mistake. You are learning how to make a burned pancake. It is only when you explore the edges of the spectrum, the place where the recipe breaks, that you truly know you've mastered it.

And so I mastered cooking.
I could make anything I wanted to make.
Until I went raw.

A chance late-night Googling on May 25, 2015 exposed me to the Dr. Morse Raw Vegan diet, and I knew it was the right choice for me. I felt challenged as a cook, and I'm still learning new things every single day!

I started RawMunchies.org to share my recipes and use this amazing experience to connect with people who are interested in healthy recipes. I thought it would be easy. I was wrong. I am challenged every day. Between my website, social media, and my beloved YouTube channel, RawMunchies, I've learned so much about fruit, vegetables, and spices.

I also found a cure for many symptoms I couldn't understand before and I have been successful at managing weight, getting naturally wrinkle-free glowing skin, and enjoying an energetic, healthy body. Yes, it's all possible.

The RawMunchies book series has something for everyone. There are smoothies, salads, noodles, sushi, raw vegan versions of junk food, and many more inspiring delicious recipes.

It's a whole new way of cooking.

Join me!

Love,

Reut

ABOUT THE DIET

THE RAW VEGAN DIET

What does it mean to be raw vegan? The raw vegan diet consists of fruits and vegetables, cooked under 42 degrees Celsius, or 108 degrees Fahrenheit, to preserve nutrients, keep enzymes in their original state, and avoid trans fats. Most raw vegans follow the diet at 80% and above.

The aim of the diet is to create a detox process, increase energy, cure disease, enjoy anti-aging benefits, and have an overall healthy lifestyle.

There are many schools in the raw vegan world, as it is currently a growing trend both in natural healing and in cookery.

DETOX

This is in no way an attempt to explain the complex workings of the human body, the different symptoms, and how they relate to the body's organs and systems, or the detox process. However, it is important to touch on the subject briefly. It is highly advisable to know more about how food and health are related and to read about the subject beyond these humble paragraphs.

Detox is the process in which the body rids itself of acids, toxins, and parasites, rebuilds cells and organs, and thus cures symptoms permanently. The raw vegan diet detoxes by nourishing the body with foods that form an alkaline environment when digested. These foods can be acidic when ingested (like lemons) but when digested they are highly alkaline. They are light, and do not waste much of the body's energy on digestion-freeing more energy to rebuild tissue. This type of cure is no different than healing from an external or internal wound.

As the body rids itself of the damaged cells, it creates symptoms ranging from easy flu-type coughing and sneezing to more major

symptoms. Many times this is hardly noticeable. However, detox can also come in a more condensed form, over a few hours to a few days, a process known as a Healing Crisis.

TWO LARGE RAW VEGAN DETOX SCHOOLS

There are as many ways to practice the diet as there are people who do so. There are even raw diets that incorporate meat, like Paleo, or diets designed for long-term veganism, like Raw Till Four.

Within the fully raw and detox oriented diets, there are two large schools: the Dr. Morse Diet and the 80/10/10 diet. The diets are similar, and both consist of mostly fruit, based on the theory that humans are frugivores, and have the most simple digestive tract, in comparison with omnivores, herbivores, and carnivores. Before spreading across the globe to cold countries, and prior to the acquisition of fire and the ability to cultivate land, humans were fruitarian, which means their main meals were made of fruits. The two diets differ on aspects relating to food combining, protein and fat ratios, and fasting.

FOOD COMBINING

The recipes in this book follow the food combination rules of the Dr. Morse Raw Vegan diet. The main purpose is to aid digestion by separating foods that require different processes. The best combination is no combination. Eating one orange after another is the easiest digestive method, since the speed and chemicals needed are consistent.

The easiest way to remember food combination is to start by separating all the melons (like melon, watermelon, cantaloupe, and papaya). Melons are the fastest digesting of all foods. Combining them with other slower digesting foods would cause a delay in the process, holding the fruit sugar in the stomach while it is fermenting, and causing alcohol levels in the blood to rise.

The next food group is the sweet fruit, for the same reasons. Waiting at least half an hour after eating sweet fruit and before eating vegetables allows the stomach to finish the process and be ready for the next meal. The remainder is slower digestive foods, like vegetables, which require at least one hour before transitioning to fast digesting foods.

Proteins (including nuts) should be separated from starches, and both should not be eaten with sweet fruit or melons. Proteins require hydrochloric acid to release pepsin and break them into amino acids, producing an acidic environment in the stomach. Starches are the opposite, and their digestion requires alkaline digestive enzymes, forming a base chemistry environment.

TRANSITIONING TO RAW

The recipes in this book are intended for everybody. There is no raw-vegan police, to the best of my knowledge, preying on unsuspecting omnivores for making burgers out of Portobello mushrooms. So everyone is welcome to have an amazing kitchen experience and learn a whole new way of cooking.

If you are considering raw vegan, it's best to find both a good raw healer or nutritionist and an enthusiastic doctor to help you with the process.

Not everyone you know is going to be supportive. When meeting with resistance, acknowledge that this is only natural, because your friends and family have known you for a long time in a certain way, and change is always difficult. You can tell them that there is sufficient medical knowledge to help you through this transition, and that you are responsible for keeping yourself healthy and avoiding any deficiencies.

It sometimes helps to think that there are religions in the world that forbid eating meat, or cultures that never introduced dairy products into their diet. Eating a plant-based diet is actually more common than we think.

THE COMMON SENSE BEHIND RAW

The reasoning behind the raw vegan diet comes from searching for the food that man would easily be able to find and eat, if left alone in nature. These are the foods designed for us. We are no different than any other animal, and just like a bear or a dove are nurtured by their environment, so are we. Two of the common reasons behind raw veganism are: no animal in nature requires the cooking of food, including meat, and dairy products are made of milk, a substance designed to nurture babies, and not even human babies. With regards to eggs, requiring cooking to avoid contamination is again a strong reason.

MORE RESOURCES

This brief summary about the diet is a good start to understand the basics of the raw vegan lifestyle. There are plenty of important resources that will give a much wider and thorough knowledge. I have listed some of them on the Raw Munchies website at www.rawmunchies.org. I hope you would find it a good place to begin.

GOING FORWARD

The recipes in this book series are only the beginning. There are many ways to explore cooking, with unlimited opportunities to try different tastes and textures. I hope this gives you enough to start on a beautiful kitchen journey and have fun creating anything from quick and easy treats to gourmet extravagance. Are you "ready to raw"?

SECRET INGREDIENTS

So how do we take a Portobello mushroom and make it taste like a juicy steak? It's all in choosing the right ingredients. This is where the magic begins. Converting a recipe is all about getting the taste right. Of course, every recipe deserves a little tweak and some ingredients get added or left behind.

When I start out to create a raw vegan version of a recipe, I look at a couple of photos to get inspired toward a certain taste. I then look at regular, vegan, and raw vegan recipes to see what ingredients are the most used.

Here are my secret ingredients. Of course, there are many more options and every person has their own favorites.

GREASY MEAT

The base for the strong meat taste is mushrooms and nuts. The strongest flavor is achieved by mixing them together.

Hazelnuts
Sunflower seeds
Walnuts

Walnuts and hazelnuts are slightly rugged in their taste, and also give a more rounded, heavy flavor. Sunflower seeds are lighter and more salty, giving a less full, more sharp taste.

Portobello mushrooms

Of the mushroom choices, this is possibly the most popular as a basis for meat. Portobello mushrooms have a steak-type texture, which they retain when dehydrated and, with a bit of seasoning, achieve a very convincing meaty taste.

Asafoetida powder

Typically used in Indian cuisine, asafoetida powder can give a very convincing greasy taste, slightly resembling egg yolk, which is commonly used in heavy meaty dishes.

Black pepper
Garlic
Herbal steak seasoning
Mustard powder
Nutmeg
Onion salt
Red onion
White onion

Garlic, onion, mustard, and black pepper are commonly used as barbecue seasoning. Nutmeg was added as a pepper substitute, and some steak seasonings have achieved a very strong greasy taste as well.

Apple cider vinegar

In a savory context, apple cider vinegar can create a taste similar to wine, which is commonly used in meat cookery.

Coconut aminos
Nama shoyu or tamari

Nama shoyu is a semi-raw soy sauce. Semi-raw as it is heated above raw temperatures, but it's unpasteurized. Tamari is a non-raw, gluten-free soy sauce and coconut aminos is a raw coconut-based soy sauce substitute. All three options have an aged taste that gives a more gourmet shade to raw vegan "meat" dishes.

Paprika
Parsley
Sun-dried tomatoes

These are often used to capture some of the less noticeable flavor notes to meat. Paprika is slightly earthy; parsley fresh; and sun-dried tomatoes resemble a ketchup nuance.

CHEEZY CHEESE

The cheese taste is achieved by using a base of nuts. Some raw vegan chefs say there is a different type of nut for each type of cheese.

Cashew nuts
Pine nuts

Cashews have the sweet and sour creamy taste that cheese normally has. Pine nuts are slightly lighter and have a saltier edge.

Thai coconut meat

For more creamy recipes, coconut meat is a great substitute. It gives a slightly sweeter direction and makes a very convincing yogurt when mixed with lemon juice, olive oil, and herbs.

Garlic

Garlic gives a slightly more crispy taste, related to harder cheeses.

Apple cider vinegar
Lemon juice

The fermentation of dairy gives a slight sour taste. For creamier cheeses, this can sometimes be achieved with lemon juice alone. Apple cider vinegar, being fermented, would give that taste more strongly.

Some cooks like to use nutritional yeast, a deactivated yeast. In my opinion, apple cider vinegar is already too fermented for more sensitive people, and to avoid fungal growth, I'd rather err on the safe side and avoid yeast, but this is my own choice.

TASTES LIKE CHICKEN

The easiest base for chicken is Thai coconut meat. It is similar in texture, simple to work with, has a mild taste and takes seasonings easily. Other types of coconut meat are less suitable. For nuggets, a base of nuts, chickpeas, and other ground substances can be used.

Thai coconut meat

The easiest chicken base to work with in terms of both texture and taste.

Chicken curry masala

This is my very favorite secret ingredient. The MDH brand from India has been using its blend of spices for generations, with the resulting taste of a spicy, slightly greasy grilled or fried chicken. Because the flavor has a non-Western direction, it adds valuable exotic taste tones.

Coconut aminos
Nama shoyu or tamari

As mentioned in GREASY MEAT, these ingredients are soy sauce substitutes. They give an aged taste, for a more gourmet direction to raw vegan "meaty" dishes.

Garlic
Rosemary
Turmeric

In the context of raw vegan "chicken," these spices would add a rugged flavor. Rosemary and turmeric would give a slightly earthy taste, turmeric being more of the home-made taste. Garlic has a more edgy sharpness.

Maple syrup
Sun-dried tomatoes

For more sweet recipes, maple syrup is the main ingredient in this book series. Both this added sweetness and the ketchup nuance of the sun-dried tomatoes enriches the taste, and takes it to the direction of chili sauce.

SCRAMBLED EGG

The flavor and texture of egg is achieved by a mixture of ingredients, some earthy to the taste and some more bland.

Thai coconut meat

This is a very easy base for egg recipes, because it bears similarity to boiled egg in texture and has a very mild taste.

Asafoetida powder
Mustard powder
Turmeric

These three spices give the direction of the egg yolk both in taste and in color. Asafoetida powder is excellent in creating the pinchy sour egg taste. Turmeric and mustard are good for the earthy yolk flavor.

Apple cider vinegar
Lemon juice

Apple cider vinegar and lemon juice can be used to help resemble the more delicate sour taste of the egg white.

ASIAN AROMA

The Asian taste goes far beyond soy sauce, even though it is the most prevalent ingredient used. It's important to mention that by Asian, the meaning is the Chinese, Japanese, and Thai food we know in the West, and not the traditional dishes.

Coconut aminos
Nama shoyu or tamari

As mentioned in GREASY MEAT, these ingredients are soy sauce substitutes. Soy sauce is both highly heated and has gluten. To maintain the fermented Asian taste of soy sauce, these ingredients can form a good base.

Apple cider vinegar

Many Asian recipes use rice as part of the dish and rice vinegar within the cooking. Apple cider vinegar gives a strong sour taste, suitable for achieving the convincing result.

Sesame oil

Though different oils are used in Asian cooking, sesame oil is the strongest taste enhancer. A few drops are sufficient to create a strong Asian, greasy gourmet taste, particularly for sweet and sour dishes.

Lemon
Lime

Lemon and lime are often used in sweet and sour dishes and give a more direct sour taste. Lime is more gentle and lemon more blunt.

Maple syrup

The main sweetener in this book series, maple syrup, is the chosen ingredient to create the sweet half of gourmet sweet and sour tastes.

Garlic
Ginger
Onion
Scallions

These Four Musketeers are often used in soups and stir-fried dishes. Garlic gives an edgy flavor, scallions are more fresh and ginger is sharp and also fresh. Onions are sometimes used to give a slightly more sweet flavor when fried over longer periods of time; a similar result can be achieved with long dehydration.

5-Spice

The spice often used to enhance Asian cuisine is the traditional 5-Spice consisting of star anise, cloves, cinnamon, Sichuan pepper, and fennel seeds.

Chili pepper
Nutmeg
Sichuan pepper

Three peppery taste creators are chili peppers for a hot taste, Sichuan peppers for a more delicate taste, and nutmeg for a lighter grounding taste.

Bamboo shoots
Bean sprouts
Bell peppers
Broccoli
Carrot
Celery
Cucumber
Mushrooms

The above list of vegetables is common in cooked and stir-fried Asian recipes. A caution is added with regards to bamboo, as many suppliers use sulfur dioxide as its preservative.

A TOUCH OF INDIA

India is a very large country, divided into many states, with different cooking traditions. Some common tastes that are used in traditional Indian restaurants in the West are listed below.

Onion
Tomatoes

These two are top ingredients in many curry dishes. Traditionally, curries are made by frying ingredients over longer periods of time. The important rule of thumb when making a raw vegan version of Indian cuisine is to dehydrate the tomatoes and onions long enough to get a more cooked taste, but with low temperature to prevent real cooking.

Garam masala

Many supermarkets sell a spice blend called "curry powder" that aims to achieve a generic curry taste. Garam masala is the traditional spice blend that achieves this result. It's much more mild, and to the Western taste buds, more authentic and exotic in flavor. It can be found in most supermarkets and Asian shops.

Asafoetida powder
Cinnamon
Coriander powder
Cumin
Garlic
Ginger
Paprika
Turmeric

The above flavors are often used in Eastern cuisine. Garlic is sharp in taste, coriander and cinnamon are soft, turmeric and cumin are earthy, ginger gives a slight fresh taste, and asafoetida is greasy in flavor.

GOURMET SWEET

The secret to getting sweet desserts to taste gourmet is to take the flavor one step away from "sweet at home" taste. Cinnamon, for example, is excellent at creating that "sweet at home" taste, and therefore is used for that purpose, and not for gourmet. In cooked cuisine, coffee is sometimes added to create a rough gourmet edge and Irish Cream or fruit liqueur are used to create a more exotic blend. Following the raw vegan diet eliminates these ingredients. But that is not to say that there isn't a much larger, rich abundance to choose from:

Vanilla

Vanilla is very round, creamy, and fine in its taste. It can add a natural well-loved flavor without risking the move toward "sweet at home."

Almond extract

Almond extract is exactly the opposite of vanilla. It's almost the taste that no one expects, in its sharpness yet exotic direction.

Lemon zest
Rose petals

Rose petals and lemon zest are a great way to shift the taste toward a larger mixture of aroma. Traditionally, we associate natural sugar with sweet fruit. Rose petals are flower-based and enrich taste in a round direction. Lemon zest comes from a non-sweet fruit and enriches the taste by adding both freshness and sharpness. A caution-to avoid pesticides, use organic, well-washed lemons.

Apple cider vinegar

To be used with caution. A few drops might give the direction of wine-based taste, but it's important to avoid any sour aroma, which can bring the flavor down.

Peach
Cherries

Like an expensive liqueur aroma, these two add the "je ne sais quoi."

EXOTIC DELIGHT

The best things come last. This one is almost all about fruit.

Cherries
Mango
Peach
Pineapple
Raspberries

Coming from tropical and warm countries, these fruits are the very definition of exotic. Mango is warm in taste; peach and cherries a bit more delicate. Both cherries and raspberries can have a strong fresh yet round flavor, and pineapple is sharp and mouth-watering.

Almond extract
Rose petals
Vanilla

These are additions that may spark exotic flavor. It's important to note they are enhancers because the best exotic taste is achieved with fruit. Almond extract has a slight sharp gourmet direction, rose petals are also gourmet but light, and vanilla is round and creamy.

SWEETENERS

There is a growing debate in raw vegan cuisine about sweeteners. It is difficult to choose the right sweetener and every person makes their choice based on health, taste, and morals.

There is no perfect choice and every ingredient has its shortcomings, which are listed below. The common used sweeteners are:

Dates -avoided by some in non-sweet fruit recipes because of food combinations
Maple syrup -plant-based and vegan, but not raw
Raw honey -healthy and light in taste, but not vegan
There are other options like raw stevia, coconut sugar, and agave, which also have debates in both directions.

The chosen sweetener for this book series is maple syrup, but the reader is encouraged to substitute with their choice.

A QUICK WORD ON DETOX

As mentioned in the previous chapter, the chief reason for raw veganism is health. It is important to remember that some ingredients are more detoxing than others. Nuts, for example, are the least detoxifying of raw vegan ingredients, followed by high-fat content foods like avocado and oils.

Not every day should be about detox. The body works in cycles, and different foods are appropriate for different days. Some people have been raw for a long time, and in the longer run can eat more heavy meals, because their body is already very clean. Others go through periods of detoxification, where some days require very light meals. There is a wide variety of fruits and vegetables in the world, rich in different nutrients that are important for the body.

The recipes in the book series are designed to serve different needs. Some recipes are directed only at detox, are made of sweet fruit only, with just a few ingredients, and low combinations. The book of smoothies consists almost entirely of such recipes.

Other recipes are directed at enjoying the wider variety of raw and a few recipes are specifically targeted for cravings of foods outside the diet, by creating a raw vegan alternative.

A NOTE ON BREAKING VEGETABLES TO PASTA TEXTURE

This note is included for the pasta salad recipes:

When sliced thin, most vegetables still maintain their crunchy texture, which in some recipes, we might want to break into a supple pasta-like texture. This method is particularly popular with zucchini recipes:

In a bowl, marinade the sliced or spiralized vegetables with olive oil and salt. You can also add apple cider vinegar, or a soy sauce substitute (Coconut Aminos, Nama Shoyu or Tamari).

RATIOS

For every 2 zucchini (or 3 cups of spiralized or sliced vegetables), add 1 tablespoon olive oil and a pinch of salt. If you're adding vinegar or soy sauce substitute, use approximately ½ teaspoon.

DELIGHTFUL CRUNCH

CASUAL CUCUMBER AND DILL

A quick and easy cucumber salad with the strong lemony-dill taste blend

Preparation time: 30 minutes

Serves Two

6 small cucumbers
1 cup dill
the juice of 3 lemons
3 teaspoons ginger powder
3 teaspoons cold-pressed olive oil
3 teaspoons nutmeg
2 teaspoons apple cider vinegar
2 teaspoons paprika
handful of pine nuts

Chop cucumbers into small slices and chop dill thin.

Mix cucumbers and dill with the rest of the ingredients and serve fresh.

MAXI MIXED LETTUCE

A quick and impressive taste blend of vegetables on a base of fresh lettuce

Preparation time: 30 minutes
Serves Two

3 cups lettuce leaves
I cup cauliflower
3 tomatoes
I orange bell pepper
I handful basil leaves
the juice of I lemon
2 teaspoons apple cider vinegar
I tablespoon cold-pressed olive oil
I tablespoon oregano
pinch salt

Chop lettuce, cauliflower, tomatoes, bell pepper, and basil leaves rough, to create a variety of textures.

Mix with the rest of the ingredients and serve fresh.

CREATIVE COLORS OF THE RAINBOW

A beautiful mix of colors for a tasty, filling crunch

Preparation time: 30 minutes

Serves Two

I avocado
I tomato
½ yellow bell pepper
½ cauliflower
½ red cabbage
the juice of 2 lemons
I handful sunflower seeds

Chop avocado, tomato, pepper, and cauliflower into large pieces and slice the cabbage thin, to create a variety of textures.

Mix with the lemon juice and sunflower seeds and serve fresh.

PERFECT PARSLEY TOMATO

A Mediterranean delicacy to build and strengthen the whole body

Preparation time: 30 minutes

Serves Two

2 cups parsley
4 tomatoes
1 onion
2 teaspoons apple cider vinegar
4 tablespoons cold-pressed olive oil
2 teaspoons nutmeg
2 teaspoons ground cumin
1 teaspoon salt

Chop parsley, tomatoes, and onion into thin slices, to create an even texture.

Mix with the rest of the ingredients and serve fresh.

PERKY PEPPERS

A charming blend of different pepper tastes to impress the senses

Preparation time: 20 minutes

Serves Two

4 different color bell peppers
the juice of 1 lemon
2 tablespoons cold-pressed olive oil
½ teaspoon dried basil
pinch salt
pinch pepper

Chop peppers rough, to create a blend of separate tastes.

Mix with the rest of the ingredients and serve fresh.

MINI MINT

A simple and powerful blend of tastes, ready to serve in a few minutes

Preparation time: 15 minutes
Serves Two

2 cucumbers
1 cup mint leaves
2 lemons

Chop cucumber into cubes, and chop mint and lemons into large slices.

Mix and serve fresh.

DELICIOUS DILL AND CHERRY TOMATO

A cherry tomato base with a strong savory blend of tastes

Preparation time: 20 minutes
Serves Two

3-4 cups cherry tomatoes
2 cups dill
the juice of **2 lemons**
2 tablespoons cold-pressed olive oil
½ teaspoon apple cider vinegar
1 tablespoon oregano
1 tablespoon rosemary
1 teaspoon nutmeg (optional)

Chop cherry tomatoes into halves and chop dill thin.

Mix with the rest of the ingredients and serve fresh.

CHUBBY CHERRY TOMATO AND WATERCRESS SPROUTS

A rich blend of tastes with a dash of fresh sprouts

Preparation time: 30 minutes

Serves Two

1 lettuce head
2 red sweet pointed peppers
4 cups cherry tomatoes
1 handful watercress sprouts
the juice of 2 lemons
2 teaspoons apple cider vinegar
1 tablespoon cold-pressed olive oil
1 tablespoon coconut aminos
1 teaspoon maple syrup
sprinkle chili flakes

Chop lettuce and peppers into large slices, and chop cherry tomatoes into halves.

Mix with the rest of the ingredients and serve fresh.

CRAZY CREAM LETTUCE

A rich creamy treat, filling and great for sharing at dinner parties

Preparation time: 30 minutes
Serves Two

CREAM

1 cup Thai coconut meat
1 cup water
the juice of 2 lemons
1 teaspoon apple cider vinegar
2 tablespoons cold-pressed olive oil
pinch salt
pinch garlic powder (optional)

SALAD

1 lettuce head

Cream
In a food processor or high-speed blender, blend Cream ingredients until smooth.

Salad
Chop lettuce into large slices. Spread cream over lettuce.

CRAZY CARROT

A strong carrot-cherry tomato blend with a fresh mix of vegetables and spices

Preparation time: 30 minutes
Serves Two

4 cups cherry tomatoes
1 carrot
1 cup basil
1 green pepper
1 cucumber
the juice of 3 lemons
2 tablespoons cold-pressed olive oil
1 tablespoon coconut aminos
1 teaspoon maple syrup
½ teaspoon cold-pressed sesame oil
2 tablespoons oregano
1 tablespoon rosemary
1 teaspoon dried basil
½ teaspoon nutmeg powder
sprinkle chili flakes

Chop cherry tomatoes into halves. Mince the carrot into fine pieces, and chop the basil, pepper, and cucumber.

Mix with the rest of the ingredients and serve fresh.

RAGING ROCKET

A quick crunchy salad, set on a strong base of peppery flavor

Preparation time: 30 minutes
Serves Two

2 cups cherry tomatoes
1 carrot
½ cup celery
1 yellow bell pepper
2 cups rocket leaves
the juice of 2 lemons
1 tablespoon cold-pressed olive oil
2 tablespoons oregano
1 teaspoon paprika
½ teaspoon dried basil

Chop cherry tomatoes into halves and chop the carrot, celery, and pepper into large pieces.

Mix with the rocket leaves and the rest of the ingredients and serve fresh.

CRUNCHY CUCUMBER

A strong warm country vegetable blend for a mix of tastes to impress the senses

Preparation time: 30 minutes
Serves Two

2 cucumbers
3 bell peppers of different colors
I cup radish
I cup dill
I cup parsley
the juice of 3 lemons
3 tablespoons cold-pressed olive oil
2 tablespoons dried oregano
I tablespoon rosemary
I teaspoon nutmeg

Chop cucumbers, peppers, radish, dill, and parsley thin, to create an even texture.

Mix with the rest of the ingredients and serve fresh.

LITTLE LEFTOVER

My absolute favorite salad, that has a little bit of everything…

Preparation time: 30 minutes
Serves Two

SALAD

4 tomatoes
½ green bell pepper
½ yellow bell pepper
½ carrot
½ cucumber
½ avocado
¼ cup dill
¼ cup basil
the juice of 2½ lemons
I tablespoon cold-pressed olive oil
I tablespoon oregano

GARNISH

I handful olives

Salad
Chop Salad ingredients into thin slices, to create an even texture, and mix well.

Garnish
Garnish with olives and serve fresh.

POPULAR SALADS FROM AROUND THE WORLD

GENIAL GREEK SALAD WITH CASHEW CHEESE

A gourmet treat from the coast of the Mediterranean, with a dash of raw vegan cheese

Preparation time: 45 minutes

Waiting time: overnight

Serves Two

CHEESE

¼ cup cashew nuts
2 tablespoons pine nuts
¼ cup water
2 tablespoons fresh lemon juice
1 tablespoon cold-pressed olive oil
pinch garlic powder
pinch salt

SALAD

2 small cucumbers
2 ripe tomatoes
2 cups lettuce
1 red or green bell pepper
¼ red onion
1 cup parsley
the juice of 3-4 lemons
2 tablespoons cold-pressed olive oil
½ teaspoon apple cider vinegar
2 tablespoons oregano
1 tablespoon rosemary
1 teaspoon za'atar or thyme
½ teaspoon paprika
½ teaspoon nutmeg
½ teaspoon cumin
pinch salt
sprinkle red pepper flakes (optional)

GARNISH

olives
lemon juice
cold-pressed olive oil

Cheese
In a food processor or high-speed blender, process Cheese ingredients until smooth.

Move the cheese into a cheese cloth. Fold and tie, then drain in the fridge overnight.

Salad
Slice cucumbers, tomatoes, and lettuce into large pieces, then cut the pepper and onion into thin slices and chop the parsley. The variety of textures is important to create an uneven blend of tastes.

Mix with the rest of the Salad ingredients.

Garnish
Garnish with olives, lemon juice, and olive oil and serve with the Cheese.

TASTY TABULI

A famous Levantine vegetarian dish, with a new cauliflower twist

Preparation time: 30 minutes
Serves Two

1 cauliflower
1 cup parsley
2 tomato
2 cucumbers
½ cup olives
4 radishes
1 cup chives
the juice of 4 lemons
2 tablespoons cold-pressed olive oil
2 teaspoons za'atar or thyme

Chop the cauliflower. In a food processor, pulse it until you reach bulgur consistency.

Chop parsley, tomatoes, cucumbers, olives, radishes, and chives into thin slices, to create an even texture.

Mix with the rest of the ingredients and serve fresh.

LOVING LETTUCE WITH GUACAMOLE DRESSING

A lettuce-based twist on a world-known Mexican treat

Preparation time: 30 minutes
Serves Two

GUACAMOLE

1 avocado
½ cup fresh coriander
the juice of 3 lemons
1 teaspoon apple cider vinegar
2 tablespoons cold-pressed olive oil
½ teaspoon mustard powder
¼ cup water
salt and pepper

½ tomato

LETTUCE BASE

2 lettuce heads

GARNISH

pine nuts
chili flakes

Guacamole
In a food processor or high-speed blender, blend all Guacamole ingredients, except the tomato, until smooth.

Chop the tomato and mix with the Guacamole.

Lettuce Base
Chop lettuce heads into large slices. Spread Guacamole over the lettuce.

Garnish
Garnish with pine nuts and chili flakes.

CREAMY COLESLAW

A true Dutch delight with a fresh, raw vegan non-fermented taste

Preparation time: 30 minutes
Serves Two

MAYONNAISE

the juice of 4 lemons
1 cup water
1 cup pine nuts
½ cup cashew nuts
3 teaspoons apple cider vinegar
2 tablespoons cold-pressed olive oil
1 teaspoon coconut aminos
1 teaspoon maple syrup
a few drops cold-pressed sesame oil
(optional)
pinch salt

VEGETABLES

1 carrot
1 cabbage

Mayonnaise
In a food processor or high-speed blender,
blend Mayonnaise ingredients until smooth.

Vegetables
Shred the carrot and slice the cabbage into
thin slices.

Mix with the Mayonnaise and serve fresh.

MAGIC MEDITERRANEAN

A quick mix of delicious cubes, famous in the countries of the Mediterranean Sea

Preparation time: 30 minutes

Serves Two

2 bell peppers in different colors
2 small cucumbers
2 tomatoes
½ onion
the juice of 1 lemon
1–2 tablespoons cold-pressed olive oil
pinch salt

Chop peppers, cucumbers, tomatoes, and onion into thin slices, to create an even texture.

Mix with the rest of the ingredients and serve fresh.

AMAZING ARABIC

An all-time Arabian favorite, fresh, savory and rich in flavor

Preparation time: 30 minutes
Serves Two

1 cucumber
3 tomatoes
1 cup parsley
the juice of 2 lemons
pinch salt
pinch black pepper

Peel the cucumber. Chop cucumber, tomatoes, and parsley into thin slices, to create an even texture.

Mix with the rest of the ingredients and serve fresh.

AMAZING ASIAN RADISH

A quick trip to the East for a rich blend of Asian tastes

Preparation time: 30 minutes

Serves Two

2 cups radish
1 cucumber
1 avocado
¼ cup scallions
the juice of 2 lemons
½ teaspoon freshly grated ginger root
½ teaspoon cold-pressed sesame oil
½ teaspoon maple syrup

Using a spiralizer julienne blade or a julienne peeler, cut radish and cucumber into long, thin slices. Chop avocado and scallions.

Mix with the rest of the ingredients and serve fresh.

GENEROUS GARDEN

A classic treat, served around the world, with a fresh and savory aroma

Preparation time: 30 minutes
Serves Two

4 cups cherry tomatoes
1 large lettuce
1 carrot
1 yellow bell pepper
½ red onion
the juice of 3 lemons
1 teaspoon apple cider vinegar
2 tablespoons cold-pressed olive oil
1 tablespoon oregano
pinch salt

Chop cherry tomatoes into halves and cut the lettuce, carrot, pepper, and onion into large slices.

Mix with the rest of the ingredients and serve fresh.

HAPPY HUMMUS

A Middle Eastern famous dressing, on a base of fresh tomatoes

Preparation time: 30 minutes
Waiting time: 8 hours
Serves Two

HUMMUS

2 cups dried chickpeas
the juice of 2 lemons
½ teaspoon apple cider vinegar
1 tablespoon cold-pressed olive oil
¾ cup water
½ teaspoon nutmeg powder
½ teaspoon cumin

½ cup parsley

FRESH VEGETABLES

4 tomatoes
4 mini bell peppers

Hummus
The most important preparation for this recipe is soaking the chickpeas overnight, or for at least 8 hours to start the sprouting process. For every cup of dried chickpeas, you will get two cups of semi-sprouted chickpeas.

In a food processor or high-speed blender, blend semi-sprouted chickpeas with lemon juice, apple cider vinegar, olive oil, water, nutmeg powder, and cumin, until smooth.

Chop parsley very thin, and mix with the Hummus.

Fresh Vegetables
Chop tomatoes and mini bell peppers into large slices.

Spread Hummus over the vegetables and serve fresh.

GOURMET SALADS

SUPER SUN-DRIED TOMATO

A rich blend of fresh and dried vegetables for a mix of tastes to dazzle the tongue

Preparation time: 45 minutes
Waiting time: 3-4 hours
Serves Two

SUN-DRIED TOMATOES

1 teaspoon scallions
1 clove garlic
½ cup sun-dried tomatoes
the juice of ½ lemon
1 tablespoon cold-pressed olive oil
1 teaspoon rosemary
1 teaspoon oregano

VEGETABLES

1½ celery ribs
1 small gem lettuce
1 avocado
3 radishes
the juice of 1½ lemons
1 tablespoon cold-pressed olive oil
½ teaspoon apple cider vinegar

Sun-Dried Tomatoes
Chop scallions and cut the garlic clove into two halves. Mix with the rest of the Sun-Dried Tomatoes ingredients.

Marinade for 3-4 hours. Then remove the garlic.

Vegetables
Chop celery, lettuce, avocado, and radishes rough, to create a variety of textures. Mix with the rest of the Vegetables ingredients.

Add the tomatoes to the Vegetables, and serve fresh.

CAPTIVATING CHICKPEAS

A fine blend of fresh vegetables, herbs, and sprouts for a rich, tasty crunch

Preparation time: 30 minutes
Waiting time: 8 hours
Serves Two

CHICKPEAS

½ cup dried chickpeas

SALAD

1 carrot
½ cucumber
3 tomatoes
1 avocado
3 cups curly leaf parsley
the juice of 2 lemons
1 teaspoon apple cider vinegar
2 tablespoons cold-pressed olive oil
½ teaspoon cold-pressed sesame oil
1 tablespoon oregano
1 tablespoon rosemary
½ tablespoon dried basil
1 teaspoon paprika
½ teaspoon turmeric
pinch salt
sprinkle chili flakes

Chickpeas
The most important preparation for this recipe is soaking the chickpeas overnight, or for at least 8 hours to start the sprouting process. For every cup of dried chickpeas, you will get two cups of semi-sprouted chickpeas.

Salad
Using a spiralizer julienne blade or julienne peeler, cut the carrot into long, thin slices. Chop cucumber, tomatoes, avocado, and parsley rough, to create a variety of textures.

Mix with the rest of the Salad ingredients and the semi-sprouted chickpeas, and serve fresh.

BABY BERALE

A loving mix of Middle East tastes with a rich vinaigrette sauce

Preparation time: 30 minutes
Serves Two

VINAIGRETTE SAUCE

the juice of 1 ½ lemons
1 teaspoon coconut aminos
1 tablespoon cold-pressed olive oil
1 teaspoon maple syrup
¼ teaspoon apple cider vinegar
½ teaspoon nutmeg
¼ teaspoon paprika
pinch mustard powder
pinch salt

SALAD

½ lettuce head
2 tomatoes
½ cucumber
½ cup corn
¼ red onion
handful olives

This salad is named after a small café that used to be in my city when I was in high school. This was my favorite salad growing up.

Vinaigrette Sauce
Mix Vinaigrette Sauce ingredients. If you like a stronger vinaigrette taste, add more vinegar and slightly more salt.

Salad
Chop lettuce rough and lay as the base for the salad.

Chop tomatoes and cucumber into small cubes and mix together. Lay on top of the lettuce leaves.

Lay corn on top of the tomatoes and cucumber.

Slice onion very thin and spread on top of the corn.

Decorate the salad with olives.

Serve with the Vinaigrette Sauce.

OVERJOYED OLIVES AND CORN

A cute mix of tastes and textures for a joyful mouthful delight

Preparation time: 30 minutes
Serves Two

4 tomatoes
½ cucumbers
½ cup dill
handful fresh basil leaves
1 cup corn
1 cup olives
the juice of 2 lemons
½ teaspoon apple cider vinegar
1 tablespoon cold-pressed olive oil
½ teaspoon maple syrup
1 tablespoon oregano
1 tablespoon rosemary
½ teaspoon nutmeg

Chop tomatoes and cucumber rough, and chop dill thin.

Mix with the rest of the ingredients and serve fresh.

CREAMY CELERY WITH AVOCADO DRESSING

A perfect combination of fresh salad and a rich creamy swirl of avocado dressing

Preparation time: 30 minutes
Serves Two

DRESSING

the juice of 3 lemons
1 avocado
¼ cup dill
¼ cup scallions
a few basil leaves
¼ cucumber
1 teaspoon maple syrup (optional)

SALAD

5 tomatoes
3 cups celery
½ cucumber
¼ cup parsley
2 tablespoons cold-pressed olive oil
1 tablespoon oregano
1 teaspoon za'atar or thyme

Dressing
In a food processor or high-speed blender, blend Dressing ingredients until smooth.

Salad
Chop the tomatoes, celery, and cucumber rough, and chop parsley thin, to create a variety of textures. Mix with the rest of the Salad ingredients.

Spread Dressing over the Salad, and serve fresh.

GREAT GREEN SALAD

A rich green salad mix with an impressive savory spicy sauce

Preparation time: 30 minutes
Serves Two

SAUCE

the juice of 3-4 lemons
2 tablespoons cold-pressed olive oil
¼ teaspoon paprika
¼ teaspoon nutmeg
pinch ginger powder
pinch salt
sprinkle of red pepper flakes (optional)

SALAD

1 large lettuce head
1 avocado
2 small cucumbers

Sauce
Mix Sauce ingredients and set aside.

Salad
Chop lettuce and avocado into large pieces, and chop cucumbers thin, to create a variety of textures.

Spread Sauce over the Salad, and serve fresh.

TENDER TOMATO PASTA

A soft mix of vegetables and pasta for a fun meal and a blend of tastes

Preparation time: 30 minutes
Serves Two

PASTA

1 zucchini

SALAD

5 tomatoes
2 bell peppers of different colors
4 cups lettuce
handful fresh basil leaves
the juice of 2 lemons
$\frac{1}{2}$ teaspoon apple cider vinegar
1 teaspoon maple syrup
1 tablespoon cold-pressed olive oil
1 teaspoon dried basil
1 teaspoon oregano
$\frac{1}{2}$ teaspoon nutmeg

Pasta
Using a spiralizer julienne or triangle blade or a julienne peeler, create pasta from the zucchini.

Salad
Chop tomatoes, bell peppers, and lettuce rough, to create a variety of textures.

Mix with the rest of the Salad ingredients and the Pasta and serve fresh.

SUPER SPROUT

A quick, delightful dish with an impressive sprout and mushroom blend

Preparation time: 30 minutes
Serves Two

1 cup closed cup mushrooms
1 bell pepper
½ cucumber
½ avocado
¼ cup dill
4 cups bean sprouts
the juice of 2 lemons
½ teaspoon apple cider vinegar
1 teaspoon Nama Shoyu or tamari
2 tablespoons cold-pressed olive oil
1 teaspoon cold-pressed sesame oil
½ teaspoon nutmeg
1 teaspoon Sichuan pepper
1 teaspoon oregano

Chop the mushrooms, bell pepper, cucumber, and avocado rough and chop the dill thin, to create a variety of textures.

Mix with the rest of the ingredients and serve fresh.

GLEAMING GREEN PASTA

A glorious green pasta dish with fresh vegetables and a dash of herbs

Preparation time: 30 minutes
Serves Two

PASTA

1 zucchini

SALAD

1 avocado
1 cup celery
1 cucumber
½ cup parsley
½ cup dill
the juice of 2 lemons
1 tablespoon cold-pressed olive oil
½ teaspoon cold-pressed sesame oil
pinch of salt
sprinkle of chili flakes

Pasta
Using a spiralizer julienne or triangle blade or a julienne peeler, create pasta from the zucchini.

Salad
Chop avocado and celery rough, and chop cucumber, parsley, and dill thin, to create a variety of textures.

Mix with the rest of the Salad ingredients and the Pasta and serve fresh.

RICH ROCKET

An impressive mix of vegetables and sprouts, on a peppery base of rocket leaves

Preparation time: 30 minutes
Waiting time: 3 days for sprouting
Serves Two

FENUGREEK SEED SPROUTS

2 tablespoons fenugreek seeds

SALAD

3 cups rocket leaves
4 tomatoes
1 avocado
the juice of 2 lemons
1 teaspoon apple cider vinegar
1 tablespoon cold-pressed olive oil
1 teaspoon maple syrup
1 tablespoon oregano
½ teaspoon basil powder
pinch salt
sprinkle chili flakes

Fenugreek Seed Sprouts
This is an optional ingredient and can be substituted by bean sprouts or other ready sprouts.

Start by washing the fenugreek seeds and then soak in water for 8 hours or overnight. Remove the water and place in a sprouting jar for 2-3 days, washing the seeds twice a day.

Salad
Lay the rocket leaves as the base for the salad.

Chop tomatoes and avocado rough, to create a variety of textures.

Mix with the rest of the ingredients and the Fenugreek Seed Sprouts, and serve fresh.

JAZZY JOSEPH

A simple but powerful cabbage salad with fresh tomatoes

Preparation time: 30 minutes

Serves Two

SALAD

2 tomatoes
I cabbage
½ onion
the juice of 2 lemons
2 tablespoons cold-pressed olive oil

OPTIONAL GARNISH

avocado

This is the salad my dad, Joseph, makes every day.

Chop tomatoes into large slices and chop cabbage and onion thin, to create a variety of textures.

Mix with the rest of the ingredients and serve fresh. I sometimes like to add some avocado to enrich the traditional salad-my own little twist.

MIRACLE MUSHROOM

A quick and impressive vegetable treat, served with dried basil and pumpkin seeds

Preparation time: 30 minutes
Serves Two

2 cups closed cup mushrooms
2 cups colorful tomatoes
1 bell pepper
1 cup parsley
1 avocado
the juice of 2 lemons
1 tablespoon cold-pressed olive oil
½ teaspoon dried basil
1 tablespoon pumpkin seeds

Chop mushrooms, tomatoes, bell pepper, parsley, and avocado rough, to create a variety of textures.

Mix with the rest of the ingredients and serve fresh.

VENUST VEGETABLES

A beautiful array of vegetables and herbs, served with a dash of cashew and pumpkin seeds

Preparation time: 30 minutes
Serves Two

SALAD

5 tomatoes
1 parsnip
1 cucumber
1 cup basil
1 cup fresh coriander
the juice of 3 lemons
1 teaspoon apple cider vinegar
1 tablespoon cold-pressed olive oil
1 teaspoon maple syrup
1 tablespoon coconut aminos
1 tablespoon oregano

GARNISH

cashew nuts
pumpkin seeds

Salad
Chop tomatoes, parsnip, cucumber, basil, and coriander rough, to create a variety of textures.

Mix with the rest of the Salad ingredients.

Garnish
Garnish with cashew nuts and pumpkin seeds, and serve fresh.

FRUIT SALADS

Bring-it-on Banana Kiwi 83

Mmm... Majestic Mediterranean Fruit 84

Beautiful Berry Pineapple 85

Mighty Mini Breakfast 86

Mega Morning Glory 87

Magical Mango Banana 88

Blackberry Bang 89

Pretty Pomegranate 90

Big Breakfast 91

Magical Mango Berry 92

Maverick Melon 93

Pineapple Punch 94

Cinnamon Creamy Banana 95

Busy Berry 96

Passionate Passion Fruit Mango 97

Fruit salads are great for breakfast or a treat!

The fruit salads in this book can easily be made into smoothies, and have appeared in their smoothie version in the book, 100 Smoothies as well.

BRING-IT-ON BANANA KIWI

A lovely canvas of contrasting flavors for a special strong taste

Preparation time: 30 minutes
Serves Two

6 bananas
6 kiwi
1½ cups strawberries

Chop the fruit rough, to create a variety of textures.

Mix and serve fresh.

MMM... MAJESTIC MEDITERRANEAN FRUIT

A warm country taste blend with a dash of Oriental fruit

Preparation time: 30 minutes

Serves Two

4 cups green grapes
6 nectarines
5 loquats
3 bananas
½ teaspoon vanilla extract
½ teaspoon rose petals
1 teaspoon maple syrup (optional)

Chop the fruit rough, to create a variety of textures.

Mix with vanilla extract, rose petals, and maple syrup and serve fresh.

BEAUTIFUL BERRY PINEAPPLE

A strong state of warm island fruit mixed with berry sweetness

Preparation time: 30 minutes
Serves Two

1 pineapple
1 cup blackberries
1 cup raspberries
4 bananas
1 teaspoon cinnamon powder
½ teaspoon almond extract
sprinkle coconut flakes

Chop the fruit rough, to create a variety of textures.

Mix with cinnamon powder and almond extract, and add a dash of coconut flakes. Serve fresh.

MIGHTY MINI BREAKFAST

A great boost for the start of day with the warm home taste of cinnamon

Preparation time: 30 minutes
Serves Two

3 cups grapes
3 apples
the juice of 7 oranges
sprinkle cinnamon

Chop the fruit rough, and mix with the orange juice.

Add a sprinkle of cinnamon and serve fresh.

MEGA MORNING GLORY

A quick and easy punch for a healthy, filling breakfast

Preparation time: 30 minutes
Serves Two

3 cups strawberries
3 cups grapes
1 mango
1 apple
1 banana

Chop the fruit rough, to create a variety of textures.

Mix and serve fresh.

MAGICAL MANGO BANANA

A journey to Southern Asia and back with a mix of Mediterranean vines

Preparation time: 30 minutes

Serves Two

1 mango
3 bananas
3 cups grapes
1 apple
½ teaspoon vanilla extract
sprinkle rose petals

Chop the fruit rough, to create a variety of textures.

Mix with vanilla extract, add a sprinkle of rose petals and serve fresh.

BLACKBERRY BANG

A European favorite mixed with warm country sweet delights

Preparation time: 30 minutes
Serves Two

1 ½ cups blackberries
3 cups strawberries
4 bananas
1 apple
sprinkle coconut flakes

Chop the fruit rough, to create a variety of textures.

Add a sprinkle of coconut flakes and serve fresh.

PRETTY POMEGRANATE

A fruit of the Himalayas with the blend of South Asian sweetness

Preparation time: 30 minutes
Serves Two

6 bananas
1 mango
1 pomegranate
1 teaspoon cinnamon
zest of 1 lemon

Chop the fruit rough, to create a variety of textures.

Mix with pomegranate seeds, cinnamon, and lemon zest and serve fresh.

BIG BREAKFAST

A sweet mix of fresh fruit for a great boost to start the day

Preparation time: 30 minutes
Serves Two

3 cups red grapes **3 cups strawberries** **4 bananas** **1 teaspoon cinnamon** **sprinkle rose petals**	Chop the fruit rough, to create a variety of textures. Add cinnamon, and a sprinkle of rose petals, and serve fresh.

MAGICAL MANGO BERRY

A winning combination of the taste of South Asian sweetness mixed with European berries

Preparation time: 30 minutes
Serves Two

1 mango 1 cup blueberries 2 cups strawberries 6 bananas	Chop the fruit rough, to create a variety of textures. Mix and serve fresh.

MAVERICK MELON

An all-melon detox salad for an energizing powerful cleanse

Preparation time: 30 minutes
Serves Two

1 melon 2 papayas 2 cups watermelon	Chop the fruit rough, to create a variety of textures. Mix and serve fresh.

PINEAPPLE PUNCH

A sweet taste of Brazil with a dash of gourmet aroma

Preparation time: 30 minutes

Serves Two

1 pineapple
4 bananas
1 cup raspberries
1 apple
zest of 1 lemon
½ teaspoon almond extract
sprinkle rose petals

Chop the fruit rough, to create a variety of textures.

Add lemon zest, almond extract, and a sprinkle of rose petals, and serve fresh.

CINNAMON CREAMY BANANA

A fine taste of berries mixed with banana sweetness

Preparation time: 30 minutes
Serves Two

4 bananas
1 teaspoon cinnamon
1 apple
1 cup blueberries
1 cup raspberries

Fork-mash the bananas and mix with cinnamon.

Chop apples, blueberries, and raspberries; mix with the bananas and serve fresh.

BUSY BERRY

A dark glandular mixture to open the path to healing

Preparation time: 30 minutes
Serves Two

3 cups strawberries
2 cups blueberries
I cup raspberries
I cup blackberries

Chop the strawberries rough.

Mix with the other berries and serve fresh.

PASSIONATE PASSION FRUIT MANGO

A simple blend that exposes the strong flavor of passion fruit

Preparation time: 30 minutes
Serves Two

6 bananas
1 mango
3 passion fruits

Chop the fruit rough, to create a variety of textures.

Mix and serve fresh.

RECIPE INDEX

INDEX

loquats 84

mango 17, 87-8, 90, 92, 97
maple syrup 14-15, 17
mayonnaise 47
MDH spice brand 14
meat flavor, creating 12-13
melon 93
milk 11
mint 27
mushrooms 12, 15, 71, 77
mustard 12, 14

nama shoyu 13-14, 15, 18
nectarines 84
nut cheeses 13
nutmeg 12, 15
nutritional yeast 13
nuts 14, 47
    cashew 13, 40, 47, 78
    for detox 17
    hazelnuts 12
    pine 13, 40, 47
    walnuts 12

olives 37, 43, 63
onion salt 12
onions 12, 15, 60
    dehydrated 15, 16
oranges 86

Paleo diet 10
papayas 93
paprika 13, 16
parsley 13, 25, 35, 40, 43, 59, 64, 72, 77
parsnip 78
passion fruit 97
pasta 68, 72
pasta texture 18
peach 16-17
peppers 15, 24, 26, 29, 33, 35, 37, 40, 48, 51, 68, 71, 77
pine nuts 40, 47
pineapple 17, 85, 94
pomegranate 90
Portobello mushrooms 12
preservatives 15
proteins 10-11

radish 35, 50, 56
raspberries 17, 85, 94-6

raw diet
    definition 10
    reasons for 11
    transitioning to 11
Raw Munchies website 11
Raw Till Four diet 10
rice vinegar 15
rocket 33, 75
rose petals 16-17, 84, 88, 91, 94
rosemary 14

scallions 15, 50, 56, 64
seasoning 12
seeds 12, 77, 78
sesame oil 15
Sichuan pepper 15
smoothies 17, 82
sourness 16
soy sauce see nama shoyu; tamari
spices 12-13, 15
starches 11
stevia 17
strawberries 83, 87, 89, 91-2, 96
sun-dried tomatoes 13, 14, 56
sweetness 16, 17

tabuli 43
tamari 13-14, 15, 18
temperature 10
texture 18
tomatoes 25, 28-9, 33, 37, 40, 43, 48-9, 51, 59-60, 63-4, 68, 75-8
    dehydrated 16
    sun-dried 13, 14, 56
trans fats 10
turmeric 14, 16

vanilla 16-17, 84, 88
vinegar 12-16

watercress 29
watermelon 93

zucchini 18, 68, 72

THANK YOU

My first thanks and the biggest hug in the world goes to Dr. Robert Morse, for writing The Detox Miracle Sourcebook, and for your life's work saving people and answering the questions of those like me, who are discovering raw vegan for the first time. Without you, this would never have happened. To Drew, Jennifer, and Shannon from the Dr. Morse Herbal Health Club and Helen from the Cotswolds Juice Retreat, who stood by me when the going was hard and believed in what I did.

To my readers, and followers, and my amazing online community that kept me enthusiastic throughout this journey. To all raw vegans and anyone who's ever made a smoothie or a salad. This is all for you.

To my supporting family and friends who accepted me the way I am, and supported me when I made this change. To Gandhali and Girish, who were very patient. You taught me how to cook traditional Indian dishes, and how to work with spices.

To Kristina Carrillo Bucaram, and her eye-changing video, which was how I first found out about this diet. To Markus Rothkranz and Cara Brotman for writing Love on a Plate, where I learned to walk my first steps in recipe conversions. You are responsible for breaking zucchini noodles. To Juliano Brotman and the video on making raw vegan meat. To Laura Miller for your amazing raw vegan tricks on the program Raw Vegan Not Gross.

To my copy editor Faith Williams, eBook formatter Dallas Hodge, photographer Julie Chalk, indexer Catherine Hookway, and cover designer Connor Jennings, who made this book series the quality that it is.

Hugs,
Reut

MORE RECIPES

www.rawmunchies.org

It's a whole new way of cooking.

THE RAW MUNCHIES BOOK SERIES

Delicious raw vegan versions of popular recipes. For everyone who wants a healthier version of pizza, burgers, sushi, and gourmet recipes.

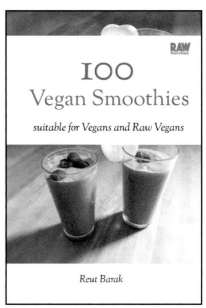

Quick and easy, energetic and mouth-watering smoothies. This book is all about health and ultra-detox. Simple food combining and few ingredients.

Quick, easy, and healthy, with a touch of style and famous salads from world cuisine. This book has both regular and ultra-detox recipes.

Easy pasta and noodles, featuring some of the most popular pasta and spaghetti recipes. This book has both regular and ultra-detox recipes.

12 VEGETARIAN SAUCES - a mini-eBook, a great companion to salads, noodles, desserts and party dips

Made in the USA
Monee, IL
14 August 2024

63902954R00064